TROLLEYBUS TWILIGHT

BRITAIN'S LAST TROLLEYBUS SYSTEMS

TROLLEYBUS TWILIGHT

BRITAIN'S LAST TROLLEYBUS SYSTEMS

JIM BLAKE

PEN & SWORD
TRANSPORT

First published in Great Britain in 2017 by
Pen & Sword Transport

An imprint of Pen & Sword Books Ltd
47 Church Street, Barnsley, South Yorkshire S70 2AS

ISBN 978 1 47386 146 6

Pen & Sword Books Ltd incorporates the imprints of Pen & Sword Archaeology, Atlas, Aviation, Battleground, Discovery, Family History, History, Maritime, Military, Naval, Politics, Railways, Select, Social History, Transport, True Crime, and Claymore Press, Frontline Books, Leo Cooper, Praetorian Press, Remember When, Seaforth Publishing and Wharncliffe.

For a complete list of Pen & Sword titles please contact
Pen & Sword Books Limited
47 Church Street, Barnsley, South Yorkshire S70 2AS England
E-mail: enquiries@pen-and-sword.co.uk
Website: www.pen-and-sword.co.uk

Design and typesetting
by Juliet Arthur, www.stimula.co.uk

Printed and bound by Replika Press Pvt. Ltd.

CONTENTS

ABOUT THE AUTHOR

I was born at the end of 1947, just five days before the 'Big Four' railway companies, and many bus companies – including London Transport – were nationalised by Clement Attlee's Labour government.

Like most young lads born in the early post-war years, I soon developed a passionate interest in railways, the myriad steam engines still running on Britain's railways in those days in particular. However, because my home in Canonbury Avenue, Islington, was just a few minutes' walk from North London's last two tram routes – the 33 in Essex Road and the 35 in Holloway Road and Upper Street – my parents often took me on these for outings to the South Bank, particularly to the Festival of Britain which was held there in the last summer they ran, in 1951. Moreover, my father worked at the GPO's West Central District Office in Holborn and often travelled to and from work on the 35 tram. As a result, I knew many of the tram crews, who would let me stand by the driver at the front of the trams as they travelled through the Kingsway Tram Subway. This was an unforgettable experience for a 4 year old! In addition, my home was in the heart of North London's trolleybus system, with route 611 actually passing my home, and one of the busiest and most complicated trolleybus junctions in the world – Holloway, Nag's Head – a short ride away along Holloway Road. Here, the trolleybuses' overhead almost blotted out the sky! Thus, from a very early age, I developed an interest in buses and trolleybuses, which was equal to my interest in railways, and I have retained both until the present day.

I was educated at my local Highbury County Grammar School, and later at Kingsway College, by coincidence a stone's throw from the old tram subway. I was first bought a camera for my fourteenth birthday at the end of 1961, which was immediately put to good use photographing the last London trolleybuses in North-West London on their very snowy last day a week later. Three years later, I started work as an administrator for the old London County Council at County Hall, by coincidence adjacent to the former Festival of Britain site. I travelled to and from work on bus routes 171 or 172, which had replaced the 33 and 35 trams mentioned above.

By now, my interest in buses and trolleybuses had expanded to include those of other operators, and I travelled throughout England and Wales between 1961 and 1968 in pursuit of them, being able to afford to travel further afield after starting work. I also bought a colour cine-camera in 1965, with which I was able to capture what is now very rare footage of long-lost buses, trolleybuses and steam locomotives. Where the latter are concerned, I was one of the initial purchasers of the unique British Railways 'Pacific' locomotive 71000 *Duke of Gloucester*, which was the last ever passenger express engine built for use in Britain. Other preservationists laughed at our group, which had purchased what in effect was a cannibalised hulk from Barry scrapyard at the end of 1973, but they laughed on the other side of their faces when, after extensive and innovative rebuilding, it steamed again in 1986. It has since become one of the best-known and loved, preserved British locomotives, often returning to the main lines.

Although I spent thirty-five years in local government administration, with the LCC's successor, the Greater London Council, then Haringey Council and finally literally back on my old doorstep, with Islington Council, I also took a break from office drudgery in 1974/5 and actually worked on the buses as a conductor at London Transport's Clapton Garage, on local routes 22, 38 and 253. Working on the latter, a former tram and trolleybus route, in particular was an unforgettable experience. I was recommended for promotion as an inspector, but rightly thought that taking such a job with the surname Blake was unwise in view of the then-current character of the same name and occupation in the On The Buses TV series and films, and so declined the offer and returned to County Hall!

By this time, I had begun to have my transport photographs published in various books and magazines featuring buses. I had also started off the North London Transport Society, which catered for enthusiasts interested in the subject. In conjunction with this group, I have also compiled and published a number of books since 1977, featuring many of the 100,000 or so transport photographs I have taken over the years.

Also, through the North London Transport Society, I became involved in setting up and organising various events for transport enthusiasts in 1980, notably the North Weald Bus Rally, which the group took over in 1984; it has raised thousands of pounds for charity ever since. These events are still going strong today.

In addition to my interest in public transport, I also have an interest in the popular music of the late 1950s and early 1960s, in particular that of the eccentric independent record producer, songwriter and manager Joe Meek. In Joe's tiny studio above a shop in Holloway Road (not far from the famous trolleybus junction) he wrote and produced Telstar by The Tornados, which became the first British pop record to make No.1 in America, at the end of 1962, long before The Beatles had even been heard of over there! When Joe died in February 1967, I set up an Appreciation Society for his music, which is still going strong today. His music has a very distinctive sound.

I also enjoy a pint or two (and usually more) of real ale. I have two grown-up daughters, Margaret and Felicity, and three grandchildren, Gracie, Freddie and Oscar, at the time of writing. I still live in North London, having moved to my present home in Palmers Green in August 1982.

INTRODUCTION

Today, many towns and cities in continental Europe have flourishing trolleybus systems, employing the latest types of vehicles as well as the latest technology needed for their operation. Yet in Britain, trolleybuses are but a distant memory, with the last traditional British trolleybus system having perished in Bradford in the spring of 1972.

How different things were when I was a youngster in the 1950s and early 1960s! I was fortunate to have been born and brought up in the heart of what was then the largest trolleybus system in the world, that of London Transport. We lived in Canonbury, with route 611 passing our home and within a ride of just five minutes or so of what must have been one of the busiest trolleybus junctions in the world, that at Holloway, Nag's Head, where eleven different trolleybus routes connecting central London with various north London suburbs converged. Therefore it was only natural that my favourite mode of road passenger transport should be the trolleybus, as it still is today.

Most British trolleybus systems, the majority of which were run by municipal authorities in the towns and cities they served, had been inaugurated during the inter-war years to replace trams. This was quite a sensible move, since much of the electrical infrastructure needed for the trams could be adapted for trolleybus operation. Unfortunately, with one or two notable exceptions such as in Cardiff, the Second World War halted the further spread of trolleybus operation for the duration. This was no more starkly obvious than in London, where most of the trams south of the River Thames survived the war as a result. When hostilities had ended, it was decided to replace them by motor buses rather than trolleybuses, and only two years after the last trams had run in July 1952, the decision was taken to replace London's trolleybuses by motor buses as

well. At this period, London Transport was Britain's biggest bus operator, and it was no surprise that all other operators followed London's lead by abandoning their trolleybus systems too. Thus just under ten years after London's last trolleybuses ran in service in May 1962, so did the last in Britain, in Bradford in March 1972.

I began transport photography just after being bought a camera for my fourteenth birthday at the end of December 1961. Appropriately, the very first photographs I took were of the last day of trolleybuses running from London's Colindale, Finchley and Stonebridge Park depots on 2 January 1962. I was lucky in that throughout most of the 1960s I travelled to many operators in England and Wales photographing their vehicles. Although there were a handful of trolleybus fleets I never managed to reach, for example distant Huddersfield, Newcastle and Teesside, I did visit most of the surviving trolleybus systems in the latter half of the 1960s. Therefore, I am pleased to be able to present many of the pictures taken on those visits in this volume. Most have never been published before.

It is tantalising, and indeed sad, to reflect that if the Second World War had not happened, or even if it had not been declared until, say, 1942 or 1943, London's tram to trolleybus conversion programme would have been completed. There would have been a huge fleet in London of about 3,000 trolleybuses – surely too vast to be abandoned in such a relatively short space of time. And if London had not abandoned its trolleybuses, other towns and cities would probably not have either! Similarly, if the surviving systems had soldiered on just a little longer into the era of efforts to reduce pollution from internal combustion motor-propelled vehicles, then maybe they would still be with us today. As things are, it pains me very much to hear Transport for London enthusing about a handful of 'electric' buses being tried out in the Croydon area as this book is being compiled in the spring of 2015. After all, when I was a lad in the 1950s, London did have about 1,800 fully electric and pollution-free buses – our splendid trolleybuses! I also cannot understand why many British towns over the past twenty years or so – including Croydon – have opted for trams rather than trolleybuses. I have nothing against trams, but surely a trolleybus system is far less costly to introduce, and the trolleybuses themselves are more flexible to operate than trams are – one of the benefits of their introduction in the 1920s and 1930s in the first place! And when so many other things are imposed on us by the European Union, why can we not follow the lead of many of its other member states by reintroducing trolleybuses to Britain's streets? I sincerely hope that, some time in the future, we may yet see the return of trolleybuses to our streets, but for now I am pleased to present this selection of photographs of how things used to be fifty years or so ago. My thanks go to Colin Clarke, Paul Everett and John Scott-Morgan for all their help in putting this book together.

Jim Blake
30 April 2015

Part One

TRAVELLING BY TROLLEYBUS REMEMBERED

Seen at snowy Craven Park on 2 January 1962, the last day of trolleybus operation in North-West London, Colindale depot's N1 class trolleybus No.1564 heads for Hammersmith on route 666. Some of the heavy snow that had fallen on New Year's Eve, which was a Sunday, is still on this trolleybus. The N1s had been new to Bow depot in the summer of 1940, and migrated to the north west when that depot converted to motor bus operation in August 1959. They had BRCW bodywork and AEC chassis.

Living as I did in the heart of North London's huge trolleybus network, with route 611 actually passing my home, I had ample opportunity to travel on them and my memories of doing so are still vivid, even though that local route perished almost fifty-five years ago.

In common with most families in my area in the 1950s and very early 1960s, my parents never owned a car (as to this day I also have not, and have never wanted to!), therefore we always travelled by public transport. There were five 'country' destinations we used to visit on summer Sundays, all of which involved riding by trolleybus! The first was either Walthamstow or Hackney Marshes, and the second the Woodford area of Epping Forest. Although bus routes 38 and 38A would take us to all of these places from nearby Essex Road, I always insisted on riding on the 581 trolleybus, which paralleled the

38A all the way from Bloomsbury to Woodford, Napier Arms and, in fact, when withdrawn in April 1959 was replaced by an increase in frequency on that bus route. The third was a trip to Hadley Wood, where we would have a picnic by the Great Northern main line while I feverishly noted the numbers of all the passing steam engines. This entailed a long ride on route 609, travelling all the way up the Great North Road from Highbury Corner to High Barnet. The fourth was an even longer ride by trolleybus, to the point furthest north from central London that they reached, Waltham Cross, for a ramble along the nearby River Lea or a visit to historic Waltham Abbey. The 679 from Highbury Corner was our mode of transport for those outings. The fifth outing, and the one we did most often, involved travelling on our very own 611 to Highgate Village for a ramble over Hampstead

Heath, often visiting the fairgrounds at Easter, Whitsun or August Bank Holiday weekends.

Other long rides we took by trolleybus were to visit relatives who lived in Barking, which entailed catching the 611 from outside our home to Old Street, and then the 665 all the way out to the east along the Commercial, West India Dock, East India Dock and Barking Roads to its terminus in Barking town centre. I well remember when that route was replaced by new Routemaster buses on route 5 in November 1959. Travelling on the new type of bus for the first time actually made me feel sick – so we came home by Underground instead! I subsequently discovered that some of these buses had an experimental form of suspension, so possibly that was the culprit. However, no matter how successful London's Routemaster buses became in later years, in my view they could never match the smooth, silent and fast running of a trolleybus!

During the last three or four years of London trolleybus operation, I visited most trolleybus depots courtesy of London Transport's 'Red Rover' tickets, which naturally involved riding on the vehicles themselves. I well remember attempting a trip to all surviving trolleybus depots, travelling only by trolleybus, on such an occasion on Saturday, 10 December 1960. Starting on a 609 from Highbury Corner, I first visited my local Highgate (previously and now again named Holloway) depot, which much to my outrage, had already lost the 611 to new bus route 271 the previously July. From there, I doubled back on a 517 to Nag's Head junction – then still fully intact – and then caught a 653 to Stamford Hill depot. Running through the heart of North London's ultra-orthodox Jewish community, this route was nicknamed 'The Yiddisher Flyer' by both crews and passengers alike, as its successor, bus route 253, still is today. From Stamford Hill, a 649 took me up the long, straight original A10 Tottenham High Road and Hertford Road to Edmonton depot, located at the end of a cul-de-sac named Tramway Avenue. From there I doubled back again, this time on a 659, to Bruce Grove station, changing to a 543 to take me to Wood Green depot. That depot was a familiar place to me, since I had relatives living in a turning directly opposite it off Jolly Butchers Hill. From there, a 621 took me on to North Finchley, Tally Ho! Corner, for the nearby

Finchley trolleybus depot. My next ride was on a 645 to Colindale depot, behind which was the 'Golgotha' of London's trolleybuses – George Cohen's scrapyard – where the majority of the fleet perished. I remember being especially saddened to see many of my 'special' trolleybuses from route 611 awaiting their fate there, of which more later. From Colindale, doubling back as far as Cricklewood Broadway, a 666 took me to my next port of call – Stonebridge Park depot, or rather Craven Park – where I had to change to a 662 for a couple of stops up the Harrow Road to the depot. Back from there I went to Craven Park, catching a 660 to Acton Vale – where disaster struck! I had intended catching a 607 from there to Hanwell depot, then a 655 down to Brentford to connect with the 657 and 667 to reach Isleworth and Fulwell depots. But when I reached Acton Vale, I was horrified to see gleaming new Routemasters running on route 207, which unbeknownst to me had converted to them from the old 607 a month before! Just as well I had visited Hanwell depot, and travelled on both the 607 and 655, the previous May. Thus I stayed on my 660 to Starch Green where I changed to a 657. That, one of the newest London trolleybuses of the Q1 class, took me all the way to Isleworth trolleybus depot near Hounslow. Then I doubled back to Busch Corner to catch a 667 down to Fulwell depot. Ironically, as things turned out, Isleworth and Fulwell would be the last London depots to operate trolleybuses just under eighteen months later. The 667 was also a Q1, and I had no idea then that just a few weeks later, these smart vehicles, some only eight years old, would start to be replaced by older trolleybuses displaced from my local area and shipped off to Spain. A 667 back to Hammersmith, then a 660 to Finchley and a 609 to Highbury Corner was my intended route homewards, but when on that cold, dark December night I spotted an RTL bus on route 73 at the traffic lights in Twickenham town centre heading for Stoke Newington, and thus passing along Essex Road near my home, I jumped off my Q1 trolleybus to catch it and thereby 'cheated' by riding on a motor bus that day after all! Still, it was no mean feat to have travelled all the way from Highbury Corner to Fulwell, via Holloway, Stamford Hill, Edmonton, Wood Green, North Finchley, Colindale and Acton, all the way by trolleybus, especially when the trolleybus to motor bus conversion programme in London was already over half completed!

I would now like to describe in detail what it was like to ride on a trolleybus some fifty-five to sixty years ago, and will choose 'my' route, the 611 and our outings 'over the (Hampstead) Heath' to do so. Owing to the steep Highgate Hill which this route traversed between Highgate (Archway) station and its terminus at Highgate Village, trolleybuses on this route were fitted with special 'run back and coast' braking, meant to safeguard against trolleybuses running backwards out of control when going up hill in the event of a power failure. Although the 611, which ran from Moorgate to Highgate Village via Hoxton and Canonbury, had a normal requirement of sixteen trolleybuses, there were actually forty of them so equipped. This was because it had been intended to run other trolleybus routes up Highgate Hill and through Highgate Village onwards to East Finchley, but the snooty residents, whose thoroughfares they and their overhead equipment would defile, successfully objected to these proposals. The special trolleybuses were the 25-strong J3 class, No.1030-1054 (EXV30-54) which were AECs with BRCW bodywork, and the 15-strong L1 class, No.1355-1369 (EXV355-369), chassisless vehicles with AEC running units and MCCW bodies. Other trolleybuses were forbidden to operate the 611, though of course the forty vehicles did work on all of the other trolleybus routes based at Highgate (Holloway) depot – for the record, the 513, 517, 609 (Sundays), 613, 615, 617, 627, 639 and 653. From as young an age as 4, I knew the trolleybuses on the 611 by heart by their registrations: EXV30-54 and EXV355-1369. There was one, however, that I never saw: EXV365 (No.1365). This unfortunate L1 was destroyed during the war when quite new, not apparently by direct enemy action, but by an electrical fire during the blackout!

Leaving our home, a block of flats called Canonbury Avenue just off Canonbury Road next door to Canonbury School, we would catch the 611 from its stop just before Canonbury Road joined St. Paul's Road at Highbury Corner. Here, until the roundabout was built there in 1958, all was one massive bomb site as a result of a 'doodlebug' V1

flying bomb landing there on 27 June 1944. As all youngsters used to do in those days, I invariably would insist on travelling upstairs, if possible, in the front seats. To do so was an unforgettable experience! Sitting above the full-width driver's cab, the sound of the trolleybus could clearly be heard – the whine of its electric motor, and the clicking of its gears. As it reached the railway bridge carrying the Great Northern main line across Holloway Road, its booms would have to be lowered to take it beneath the bridge, which would cause a loud rumbling sound. A similar rumbling would take place as it felt its way through the intricate junction of trolleybus overhead a short distance further on, at the Nag's Head. I well remember when, as a small boy, I used to think it was the rumbling of an approaching thunderstorm and would become really upset, thinking our ramble over the Heath would be ruined! Similar rumblings would occur as we passed beneath the junction for the spur into Pemberton Gardens where the trolleybuses reached their depot, just off Holloway Road north of Upper Holloway station, and then again at Archway station where routes 517, 609 and 617 parted company with the 611 to go up Archway Road towards Finchley. Then would come the steep climb up Highgate Hill, which was quite a feat for the trolleybuses, especially on Bank Holidays when they would be full of people heading for the Hampstead Heath fairgrounds. They were so busy, in fact, that extra trolleybuses would run – which actually carried the word 'EXTRA' instead of their route number in the front blind box. Then, finally, we would reach the terminus, a turning circle off Highgate High Street in South Grove, which just had space for two trolleybuses to stand alongside one another. That terminus is still used today by bus route 271, which replaced the 611 outright in July 1960, and the original trolleybus shelter erected when the 611 was introduced in December 1939 is still in use! The journey homewards was equally exciting, when our trolleybus would sweep down Highgate Hill, revealing in the distance a panoramic view of the City of London with St. Paul's Cathedral as its centrepiece, before horrible modern tower blocks ruined the view!

Of course, travelling by trolleybus was not without its mishaps. Once, we had barely started

Routes 660 and 666 ran together all the way from Cricklewood Broadway to Hammersmith, starting at North Finchley and Edgware respectively. However, trolleybus No.1529 has been curtailed at Craven Park on the 660; its driver converses with the point inspector seen on the left. This location was also the crew-change point for trolleybuses working these routes from nearby Stonebridge Park depot. No.1529 was the last of the 150-strong L3 class delivered in 1939/40, which were chassisless vehicles having AEC units and MCCW bodywork. Many of these entered service at Poplar depot in the summer of 1940, and moved to north and North-West London when Routemaster buses replaced them in November 1959. This particular one was unusual in that it had sliding windows rather than the usual half-drop opening ones. Although some of this class displaced on this occasion survived to run for another few months at Fulwell, No.1529 was withdrawn. The two other trolleybuses seen in this view are N1s. Of note above them are the thicker trolleybus overhead wires, which are 'feeder' wires taking current to the running wires.

Around the corner in Harrow Road, N1 class trolleybus No.1621 is for some reason out of service with its booms down, as No.1651 overtakes it on route 662 bound for Paddington Green. This is one of the small class of N2 type trolleybuses delivered in 1940. Only 25 strong, these were AECs with Park Royal bodywork, constructed just a short distance away from where these two were based at Stonebridge Park depot. The thicker rainstrips above their front upper-deck windows immediately identified them. Both the N1 and N2 classes became extinct upon this conversion.

Another Stonebridge

Park trolleybus, N1 No.1619, heads for Hammersmith beneath the 'frog' where route 662 parted company with the 660 and 666 at Craven Park. The building on the extreme right of this picture was the London Transport staff canteen for crews changing over on trolleybuses from this depot at this point.

our journey to Highgate on the 611 when, before the first stop along Holloway Road, there was a loud bang, and our trolleybus shuddered to a halt. It had become dewired and one of the collector shoes that gripped the overhead wires at the end of its booms had fallen off and landed on the pavement! If it had landed on someone's head they would surely have been seriously injured, if not killed. As it was, the crew were unable to fix it, so we had to wait to be transferred to the one following a few minutes behind. Though it was not the case on this occasion, trees coming into leaf in the spring and early summer were a menace to trolleybuses. There were a couple of large chestnut trees in the playground of my junior school, Canonbury, which was next door to our block of flats. These always seemed to foul the overhead for southbound trolleybuses on route 611, which on many occasions were dewired there. For some reason, one of the J3s (No.1045, EXV45) always seemed to be the victim. Once, it dewired so

violently that it actually brought the wires down, including those bringing the electric current to them from a nearby feeder pillar. It happened in the evening rush hour, bringing complete chaos to busy Canonbury Road and causing the trolleybuses to have to run at snail's pace on their batteries from Canonbury Square to Highbury Corner. If only I had had a camera to record the scene, especially as it was possible to look down on them from the roof of our block of flats! London Transport had a fleet of tower wagons to attend to such problems with the overhead, as well as some converted pre-war STL buses used as tree loppers. Such dewirements were the most common problem with trolleybuses. The most spectacular dewirement I ever saw also involved a 611. In 1958, the new roundabout was built at Highbury Corner where the bomb site had been, involving re-routing the trolleybus overhead. As a result, 609s and 679s heading south, bound for Upper Street and the Angel had a parallel set of

At the same point, with the LT canteen on the left, N1 class trolleybus No.1558 works Stonebridge duty SE1 on route 660, bound for North Finchley. The 70-seater is surprisingly empty on this Tuesday afternoon, perhaps because of the freezing weather? Note the sticker in the second from rear window on its lower deck – this is the notice saying that tomorrow the trolleybuses will be replaced by new bus routes 245 (for the 645), 260 (for the 660), 266 (for the 666) and an extension of the existing 18 for the 662. The notices were nicknamed 'yellow perils' as they were printed on bright yellow paper and also affixed to the trolleybus traction standards. Today, all of these bus routes still exist, albeit in shortened forms.

It is the last day of London's trolleybuses, Tuesday, 8 May 1962, and I have 'bunked' school for the afternoon to travel across from my home in Canonbury to Hammersmith to photograph them. I can do this in one hit, by RTL bus on route 73! Here, in Hammersmith Grove, L3 class chassisless MCCW-bodied AEC trolleybus No.1413 from Fulwell Depot awaits departure on route 667 to Hampton Court as its clippie chats to the driver. The Routemaster bus behind is on either route 260 or 266 which replaced the trolleybuses seen above in January. I rode on No.1413 to Fulwell depot, and by chance it was also the trolleybus I rode homewards on, thus having the dubious distinction of being the last London trolleybus I ever rode on in service. This was quite appropriate, since it had previously been based at my local Highgate depot, but had been transferred across to Fulwell early in 1961 to replace the newer Q1 class trolleybuses based there. These were built only between 1948 and 1953 and had originally been meant to survive until about 1970, but buyers were found for them in Spain as we shall see later.

wires to those of the southbound 611, taking them along the first sections of St. Paul's Road and Canonbury Road on the eastern side of the roundabout, before going around it and crossing the 611's northbound wires and turning left into Upper Street. One morning, just a few days before the 611 was withdrawn on 20 July 1960, I was approaching this junction on my way to school in Highbury Grove. Here I witnessed the rare spectacle of one trolleybus overtaking another, which of course was possible with these two sets of parallel wires, with a

611 on the outside wires overtaking a 609 on the inner wires. The driver of the 611 was obviously having a last fling before the route's withdrawal, but took the sharp corner outside the Hen & Chickens pub too fast, and was thereby dewired. The 611's flailing booms both came off the wires, also knocking those of the 609 (which was neck and neck with it) off the wires, so violently that the 609's nearside boom was broken! Once again, if only I had had a camera with me! Trolleybuses were also renowned for their fast acceleration, and I once

nearly came to grief as a result of this. I had just visited Tottenham Bus Garage early in 1961, when I spotted a southbound 679 – my trolleybus home – on the other side of the High Road. I managed to jump aboard as it pulled away from its stop, but its acceleration was so fast that I ended up being wrapped around the grab-pole in the centre of its platform and almost became strangled by the chord of the duffel bag on my shoulder! I managed to hang on until it stopped at Ward's Corner, when I clambered inside and found a seat, but I shall never forget that experience!

I was also fortunate to have been able to ride on trolleybuses outside London; notably on the runs from Manchester Piccadilly to Ashton-Under-Lyne and Stalybridge and back, and from Cardiff Corporation's Newport Road trolleybus depot in to the city centre, as well as from the town and city centres of the other fleets, illustrated in this book,

that I visited out to their depots. It was also relatively easy to find where their depots were if you were a stranger in town, as their overhead wires inevitably led to them! I well recall as a lad of just thirteen and a half travelling down to Brighton and walking all the way from Old Steine, following the overhead all the way out to the Corporation's depot on Lewes Road. How sad I never had a camera, but I was lucky to have seen those trolleybuses at all, since the system was abandoned shortly afterwards at the end of June 1961. I also, most unfortunately, visited Ipswich and Portsmouth just too late to see their trolleybuses in action, just a few days after these systems were abandoned in the summers of 1963. Indeed, the withdrawn vehicles were still in their depots.

All these years later, it seems a different world when many of our towns and cities were served by trolleybuses – as indeed it was!

Part Two

TROLLEYBUS TWILIGHT

Beneath the web of overhead, class L3 trolleybus No.1432 runs out from Fulwell depot to take up service on route 667 for the evening rush hour for the last time. In common with all but one of London's trolleybus depots, this had originally been a tram depot. It is one of a handful of these still in use as a bus garage today. Route 667 was replaced by new bus route 267 the next day, and this still exists today though also in shortened form.

Fulwell depot had entrances and exits at either end, and at its other (eastern) one, L3 No.1489 has managed to dewire itself as it sets off to take up service on Kingston circular route 603! Today, two different London bus operators are based at Fulwell, using one set of entrances and exits each.

Passing Fulwell depot's eastern entrance/exit in Stanley Road, L3 No.1446 heads for Tolworth on route 601, which started at nearby Twickenham. Next day, new bus route 281 replaced the 601 and continued from Twickenham to Hounslow. It still runs today.

Fellow class L3 trolleybus was chosen to be the very last one of all, and is suitably decked out and posed outside Fulwell depot. It performed the last rites there when it ran in from service on route 601 in the early hours of Wednesday, 9 May.

Seen at the rear of Fulwell depot, L3 trolleybuses 1477, 1518 and 1519 will never run again. Note the young 'bus spotter', complete with school uniform, one of many – including myself – who invaded the depot on that fateful day. Usually, we were swiftly ejected from London Transport premises, but on this occasion no one seemed to worry. My headmaster did, however, since my absence at our weekly cricket sessions that afternoon was noted! Summoned to him next morning, I only escaped the cane because I was useless at any form of sport and he appreciated what the last day of London's trolleybuses meant to me! Indeed, I was actually in tears as I walked up Canonbury Road after my ride home on route 73 late that evening!

The operator closest to London which had trolleybuses was Maidstone Corporation. On 30 April 1965, their No.72 is a 1946 Sunbeam W with BTH equipment and Northern Coachbuilders bodywork. By now it is one of the oldest trolleybuses in the fleet still carrying original bodywork, and is seen at Barming. Happily, it survives today at the Sandtoft trolleybus centre.

Maidstone Corporation trolleybus No.58 is another Sunbeam W. New in 1944, its original utility body was replaced by this new Roe 62-seat body only in 1960. Despite this, the Maidstone trolleybus system closed in April 1967.

A visit to Nottingham on 8 August 1965, finds their 1952 BUT 9641T Brush-bodied trolleybus No. 597 working route 40 in Lower Parliament Street.

Sadly, the trolleybus system here was now in decline and would be abandoned in June 1966. Two condemned trolleybuses of the same type as No.597 are seen amongst a group in the yard of Lower Parliament Street depot. They should have had several more years' life in them.

Another visit to Nottingham on 3 October 1965 finds the Corporation's 1949 BUT 9641T Brush-bodied 70-seater trolleybus No.518 passing beneath a splendid web of overhead outside Nottingham City Hall. Route 40 was converted to motor bus operation shortly after this picture was taken.

TROLLEYBUS TWILIGHT • 27

Nottingham trolleybus No.583, a similar BUT with Brush bodywork built in 1952, stands at the city centre terminus of route 36A. This trolleybus was withdrawn a few days after this picture was taken.

Reading Corporation had an extensive trolleybus system, which was still intact when this view of their No.173, a Park Royal 68-seater Sunbeam S7 six-wheeler built in 1950, was taken at St. Mary Butts on 17 October 1965.

Such was Reading's faith in trolleybuses that their original batch built in 1939 was replaced in the summer of 1961 by new trolleybuses! One of these, No.184, stands outside their Mill Lane depot beneath a web of overhead. It is a Burlingham-bodied Sunbeam F4A, whose 68-seat forward-entrance body could have been adapted for one-man operation. When Reading's system was abandoned in November 1968, some of these splendid trolleybuses saw another couple of years' service on Teesside.

A most unlikely place to find trolleybuses was Epsom Downs, but here on Derby Day, 1 June 1966, is this former Huddersfield Corporation trolleybus, which has suffered the ignominy of being converted for use as a gentlemen's toilet! The lower deck was used as the actual toilet, whilst the cisterns and water tanks were on the upper deck.

There was one for the ladies too, presumably with similar arrangements. It has attracted a long queue here, waiting patiently in the rain. The vehicles were owned by Epsom & Ewell Urban District Council.

Unfortunately, trolleybus operation in Nottingham came to an end on 30 June 1966. Here on their final Sunday, 26 June 1966; their 1950 Brush-bodied BUT 9641T 70-seater No.521 is seen in the city centre.

Derby was another East Midlands city to operate trolleybuses. Here on the following Sunday, 3 July 1966, their No.494, a Brush-bodied Sunbeam F4 56-seater, is seen in the city centre.

Somewhere along Derby's route 55, trolleybus No.225 has suffered a dewirement at a junction and its crew have had to alight to remedy things. This is a 1952-built Sunbeam F4 with Willowbrook 60-seat bodywork.

Sister trolleybus No.226 works route 32 towards Derby Midland Station along Uttoxeter Road.

Derby's newest trolleybuses were a batch of Sunbeam F4As delivered as recently as 1960 with Roe 65-seat bodywork. That did not save them from the scrapyard when the system was abandoned in September 1967! Here we see No.237, which, however, was rescued for preservation.

A visit to Manchester on 16 July 1966 finds Corporation trolleybus No.1357 working route 215 to Audenshaw. This is a BUT 9612T with Burlingham 70-seat bodywork dating from 1955. Its rather unkempt appearance and bent booms show that the end is near!

Back in Manchester again on 6 August 1966, 1956 Bond-bodied BUT trolleybus No.82 heads for Stalybridge on route 218 when seen at Piccadilly.

At Stalybridge Bus Station, Manchester City 1955 Burlingham-bodied BUT 9612T trolleybus No.1301 sets off for home, leaving one of the Ashton vehicles on the stand. By now, this was the only instance where trolleybuses from two different operators shared the wires, which, oddly enough, were owned by SHMD (Stalybridge, Hyde, Mossley and Dunkinfield Transport & Electricity Board) in this area. Both of these trolleybus systems were abandoned at the end of December 1966.

Wolverhampton Corporation still operated trolleybuses at this period, and a trip to the city on 25 July, a 66 finds their No.432, one of the oldest still in service, working route 58 from Wolverhampton to Dudley via Sedgley. Its badly bent booms illustrate how the system is being run down. This trolleybus is a Sunbeam W, new in 1945, whose original utility body was replaced by a new Roe one, seating 60, in 1958. Livery is green and yellow.

No.444 of the same type dates from 1947, but was rebodied by Roe as late as 1962. It is seen at the city centre terminus of route 58. Note how, behind the trolleybus, the overhead is suspended by a bracket attached to the wall of a building, rather than being held in place by traction standards.

Also of the same batch and working route 58, trolleybus No.441 contrasts with modern buildings in Wolverhampton city centre.

With the demise of Wolverhampton's trolleybuses on the horizon (it happened early in March 1967), those damaged in accidents were not repaired. 1945 Sunbeam W No.421 (rebodied in 1960) appears to have met a very nasty end, and it is to be hoped its driver survived the crash! It is dumped outside the Corporation's depot in Cleveland Road, Fallings Park.

Dumped at the same location are three different types of Wolverhampton trolleybuses: No.430 of the same batch as the one above, No.478, a Sunbeam W with Park Royal 54-seat bodywork new in 1947, and No.416, another utility Sunbeam W, new in 1944, that had been rebodied by Park Royal in 1952.

Looking even more forlorn, Wolverhampton No.652 was one of the last trolleybuses built for the Corporation, a Guy BT whose chassis was built at their nearby Fallings Park Works in 1950, and fitted with Park Royal 54-seat bodywork. Happily, No.654 of this batch survives in preservation.

With one of its stunted booms pointing skywards, this is Wolverhampton No.406, a 1944 utility Sunbeam W rebodied by Park Royal in 1952.

No.416, also a wartime Sunbeam W that had been rebodied by Park Royal in 1952, is dumped at Fallings Park, too. The reason these hulks remained at the depot is that they provided spare parts to keep surviving trolleybuses in service.

A second West Midlands municipal operator to operate trolleybuses at this period was Walsall Corporation. Here at their depot on 23 October 1966, No.333 is a 1946 Sunbeam W with heavily rebuilt utility Roe bodywork. It now awaits disposal, reflecting the sad fact that this system too was now in terminal decline.

Walsall's newest trolleybuses were a batch of twenty-two BTH-equipped Sunbeam F4As built between 1954 and 1956 with bulbous-looking Willowbrook 70-seat bodies. No.872 was the last of this batch and is seen with two others in Walsall Bus Station. The Corporation did purchase second-hand trolleybuses from other operators whose systems had been abandoned, as late as 1963, but all of these were in the depot on this Sunday when I visited the town! This system lasted quite late, not being abandoned until October 1970. Fortunately, though, No.872 was rescued for preservation by the British Trolleybus Society.

Built only in 1955, Manchester Corporation Bond-bodied BUT 9612T trolleybuses 1339 and 1328 have been dumped at their Hyde Road yard since 1964. No.1339 still bears the earlier Corporation livery with cream upper-deck window surrounds. They are seen on 10 December 1966, three weeks before the system was finally abandoned.

Of the same batch, doomed trolleybus No.1323 appears to have been vandalised. The people seen in the background of this picture are also enthusiasts, who with myself were on a tour of Manchester Corporation routes and depots to mark the withdrawal of their last Crossley double-decker motor buses.

One of the Crossleys, No.2072, accompanies trolleybus No.1305 in the disposal yard. It is ironic that, as Manchester Corporation was withdrawing its last trolleybuses, the West Coast main line connecting the city with London and Birmingham had recently been electrified. Its overhead equipment may be seen in the background on the left of this picture.

Still very much alive is Bournemouth trolleybus No.295, a Sunbeam MF2B with Weymann 63-seat dual-entrance bodywork new in 1959, seen at The Square terminus on a gloomy Sunday, 15 January 1967. I travelled down to Bournemouth that day behind Bulleid West Country 'Pacific' No.34098 *Templecombe* to visit both the engine shed and the Corporation's Mallard Road trolleybus depot.

At the Mallard Road depot, similar trolleybuses 258, 260 and 257 are amongst a group that have been withdrawn which, sadly, will never run again despite being only eight years old! They are a batch of twenty Sunbeam MF2Bs new in 1958.

Some of the older six-wheelers are still dumped at the depot too. Here, No.238 nicely shows off the dual entrance/exit arrangement of this type. They are BUT 9641Ts with Weymann dual-entrance bodies new in 1950.

Another view of some of Bournemouth's last six-wheel trolleybuses makes a depressing sight at Mallard Road depot.

Sunday, 5 March 1967 was the last day of trolleybus operation in Wolverhampton. Here, their 1947 Sunbeam W No.451 is seen in the city centre on route 58 bound for Dudley. These trolleybuses were given new Roe 60-seat bodies built only between 1958 and 1962 – what a waste!

To mark the demise of Wolverhampton's trolleybuses, preserved Rotherham Corporation Daimler CTC6 No.44 did a trip to Dudley and back over route 58. Built in 1950, originally with a single-deck East Lancs body, it was given a new Roe 72-seat double-deck body in 1959 – only to be withdrawn when Rotherham's system was abandoned just six years later in October 1965!

At the Corporation's Cleveland Road depot, No.449 of the same batch as No.451 seen above has just run in, probably for the last time. This is a typical former tram and trolleybus depot; note the stonework sign above the left-hand entrance, which states 'Municipal Tramways Car Depot'.

This group of Wolverhampton trolleybuses, with No.440 and No.437 in the foreground, dumped on waste ground behind the depot, will never run again. The one nearest the camera has had its lower-deck windows smashed by vandals, but now it doesn't matter anymore!

A visit to Cardiff on 8 April 1967 finds the Corporation's trolleybus No.220 amongst a group parked outside their Newport Road depot. This is one of twenty BUT 9641T six-wheelers with East Lancs 67-seat bodywork delivered in 1948.

A newer Cardiff trolleybus is No.280, one of thirteen BUT 9641Ts with East Lancs 72-seat rear-entrance bodywork new in 1955. It is seen at Wood Street terminus near Cardiff General Station. Sadly, this trolleybus system was abandoned in January 1970.

Also at the Wood Street terminus, Cardiff trolleybus No.227 is another of the 1948 batch of BUT 9641Ts with East Lancs bodywork. Another of the same batch follows.

Trolleybus No.273 is also a BUT 9641T, but has Bruce Coachworks 67-seat bodywork. It is one of ten delivered in 1950.

Cardiff trolleybus No.251 is a BUT 9641T with Bruce bodywork, one of fourteen delivered in 1949. It is seen in heavy traffic on route 8.

Another look at 1955 East Lancs-bodied BUT 9641T No.280, carrying a good load of passengers out of the city centre on route 10B.

On sister route 10A, 1950 Bruce-bodied BUT 9641T No.273 is the next one along behind No.280, but appears to be very lightly loaded.

No.230, last of the batch of twenty East Lancs-bodied BUT 9641T 67-seaters built in 1948, heads out of Cardiff city centre on route 8. This view shows clearly how these trolley-buses were originally dual entrance/exit, but their front entrance/exits have by now been removed.

No.253, another of the 1949 Bruce-bodied BUT 9641Ts, heads into Cardiff city centre on route 10B bound for Wood Street.

At the same spot, trolleybus No.251 of this same batch returns on route 8.

No.287, the last of Cardiff's final batch of East Lancs-bodied BUT 9641T 72-seaters delivered in 1955, crosses the River Taff on route 10B.

Cardiff trolleybus No.249, a BUT 9641T with East Lancs bodywork, passes Sophia Gardens on route 8. Note how it has a notice in its windscreen advertising Billy Smart's Circus, which is also promoted on the traction standard beside it and is being held nearby.

Back in Cardiff city centre, 1948 East Lancs-bodied BUT 9641T No.216 passes the Queen's Hotel.

Not far behind, No.250, one of just five East Lancs-bodied BUT 9641Ts built in 1949, works route 1. The rest of this batch of thirty BUTs delivered in 1949/50 had Bruce Coachworks bodywork, like the one in the next photograph.

Also in Cardiff city centre, trolleybus No.271, another BUT 9641T but with Bruce Coachworks bodywork, built in 1950, works route 1. This system was unusual in that it was not introduced, replacing Cardiff's trams, until 1942 – at the height of the Second World War, at a time when London's tram to trolleybus conversion programme was in abeyance due to the war, never to be completed after it.

The next operator to lose trolleybuses was Maidstone Corporation, just six weeks after Wolverhampton Corporation! On their last day of service, 15 April 1967, No.58 is a wartime Sunbeam, originally bodied by Park Royal in 1944 and given a new Roe body only in 1960. It is seen in heavy traffic in the town centre.

Maidstone Corporation No.64 is a 1946 Sunbeam W with BTH equipment and its original Northern Coachbuilders bodywork. It heads for Barming, Bull Inn, also on the last day of this system's operation.

Another trolleybus system on the Western Region main line still active in 1967 was Reading, just forty miles or so west of London! On 29 April 1967, Reading Corporation's No.190 is one of a batch of twelve Burlingham forward-entrance 68-seat Sunbeam F4As built only in the summer of 1961 to replace earlier vehicles. It heads along Broad Street bound for Tilehurst. Sadly, this system was abandoned in November 1968.

In the Corporation's Mill Lane depot is a line up of three Sunbeam S7 six-wheelers with Park Royal 68-seat bodywork, built in 1950. Nos 177, 173 and 170 are part of a batch of ten. One of the 1961 F4As joins them on the extreme right.

Also in the depot is No.140, a 56-seat BUT 9611T four-wheeler, also with Park Royal bodywork. Twenty of these were delivered to Reading Corporation in 1949.

An older Reading Corporation trolleybus seen that day is their No.113, an AEC 661T with Park Royal 56-seat bodywork that had been new in May 1939, and replaced by the new Burlingham-bodied Sunbeams seen above in the summer of 1961. It is seen undergoing restoration at the premises of coach operator Smiths of Reading and had been rescued by the British Trolleybus Society.

Seen behind Reading 113 at Smith's is South Shields Corporation trolleybus No.204, also in the care of the British Trolleybus Society. This is a Karrier E4 with Weymann 55-seat bodywork, and was new in May 1937. The South Shields system had been abandoned in April 1964.

Another trolleybus rescued for preservation at this period is Derby No.172. It is a Sunbeam W with Weymann 56-seat utility bodywork, new in August 1944. It is seen here on tow on Brighton seafront after attending the HCVC (Historic Commercial Vehicle Club) London-Brighton road run and rally on 7 May 1967.

Epsom & Ewell's ex-Huddersfield Corporation trolleybuses are still in use as public conveniences at Epsom Downs on Derby Day, 7 June 1967. In this view of the Ladies' one, a 'customer' is just visible on the upper deck, implying that cubicles were installed upstairs too on the Ladies' versions. Is the gentleman in the foreground waiting while his wife uses the facilities? The ground looks rather waterlogged, so it is to be hoped the poor old trolleybus is not leaking!

A trip to Derby on 2 July 1967 finds 1953 Willowbrook-bodied Sunbeam F4 60-seater No.229 passing Roe-bodied Sunbeam F4A No.239, a 65-seater built only in 1960, whose booms have had to be lowered to enable No.229 to do so at Market Place terminus.

Derby No.242, another 1960-built Sunbeam F4A with Roe 65-seat bodywork, arrives at the Market Place. This trolleybus system would perish in September.

A last look at Derby Corporation's trolleybuses: Willowbrook bodied Sunbeam F4 60-seater No.221, at the Market Place terminus, is one of twenty built in 1952/53.

A trip to Bradford on 7 October 1967 sees one of many second-hand trolleybuses in the Corporation's fleet, No.782, a Karrier W that had been new to Llanelli in 1946 and acquired by Bradford Corporation in 1952 after South Wales Transport had taken over and abandoned the Llanelli system. It was given a new East Lancs 63-seat body in 1956. This view sees it at Forster Square.

Also rebodied by East Lancs, but with a forward-entrance body in 1959, trolleybus No.707 is a Karrier W originally new to Bradford Corporation in 1945 with Roe wartime utility bodywork. Vehicles of this batch survived until the very end of trolleybus operation in Bradford in March 1972.

Outside Bradford Corporation's Thornbury depot, trolleybus No.845 is a Sunbeam F4 that had been new to Mexborough & Swinton in 1950. When that system was abandoned in March 1961, it was sold to Bradford and given new forward-entrance East Lancs bodywork seating 69 passengers in 1962. There were four such vehicles, which had originally been single-deckers. Bearing the last double-deck trolleybus bodies ever built for use in Great Britain, all four are now preserved. This one is at Sandtoft trolleybus centre.

Trolleybus No.729 has travelled through the overhead wires junction outside Thornbury depot too fast, resulting in this spectacular dewirement! It is a Karrier W, new to Bradford in 1946, and given a new forward-entrance East Lancs body in 1959.

Since the dewirement took place outside the depot, help was soon at hand! A tower wagon has been summoned, allowing damage to the trolleybus' booms to be repaired. No.729's crew look on as this is carried out.

Although Bradford would be the last British fleet to operate trolleybuses, in March 1972, some of them were already being withdrawn in 1967. One such is No.798, a 1951 BUT 9611T acquired from St Helen's Corporation in 1958 and still carrying its original East Lancs 56-seat bodywork. It is out of action at the rear of the depot.

Also withdrawn in the depot yard is No.781, another of the ex-Llanelli trolleybuses rebodied by East Lancs only in 1958.

Another ex-Llanelli trolleybus, No.775, is seen inside the depot. Bradford acquired ten of these in all. It is of note that motor buses were kept alongside trolleybuses here, as evidenced by the AEC Regent V on the right.

Changing crew outside the depot is trolleybus No.789, a Karrier W which had been new to Darlington Corporation in 1944, originally with utility bodywork. Once again, it gained new East Lancs bodywork when acquired by Bradford Corporation, in this case a forward-entrance version seating 70.

Beneath a splendid web of trolleybus overhead at Forster Square in the city centre, Bradford Corporation trolleybus No.592 heads for Clayton on route 37. This is one of ten AEC 661Ts built in 1941/42 that were acquired from Notts & Derby in 1953, and given new East Lancs bodies in 1958. Three other Bradford trolleybuses are visible in this picture. If only we could see such sights on Britain's streets today!

At the same location as the previous picture, this time on route 45 bound for Wibsey, is No.778, another of the ex-Llanelli trolleybuses.

On the same route is No.758, one of few Bradford trolleybuses not to have received new East Lancs bodies! It is one of eight BUT 9611Ts built new for the Corporation in 1950/51 with Weymann 59-seat bodywork, and after withdrawal was preserved by the British Trolleybus Association.

Also carrying its original bodywork, built by East Lancs, No.794 is another 1951 BUT 9611T 56-seater acquired from St. Helen's Corporation in 1958. Although most of this batch survived until 1971, this one was withdrawn in 1968.

Another former Darlington Corporation trolleybus to be acquired by Bradford Corporation is No.834, which was given this smart new East Lancs body only in 1962. It was new in 1949, but for some reason sold to Doncaster Corporation in 1952. Originally fitted with East Lancs 56-seat bodywork, it was sold to Bradford in 1960. As may be seen, its forward-entrance body could easily have been adapted for one-man operation. Here it climbs out of Bradford city centre bound for Buttershaw. Though with some of the most modern bodywork in Bradford's trolleybus fleet, all of this batch were withdrawn in 1971, some months before the end. Luckily, this one was rescued for preservation and is at Sandtoft trolleybus centre, near Doncaster, today.

Still with its original Weymann 59-seat bodywork, Bradford trolleybus No.753 is a BUT 9611T new in 1950, one of a batch of eight. This one remained in service until 1970.

A last look at Bradford's trolleybuses: No.588 is another of the ten AEC 661Ts, new in 1941/42 to the Notts & Derby system, from whom they were acquired in 1953. They were given new East Lancs bodies in 1958.

Next day, 8 October 1967, I visited another trolleybus system – that at Reading. The Corporation's 1950 Park Royal Sunbeam S7 68-seat six-wheeler No.174 passes beneath a web of overhead in the town centre. Twelve of these were delivered to Reading, and this one survives in preservation today.

My main reason for visiting Reading that day was to see the splendidly preserved London Transport C2 class trolleybus No.260 touring their system. This view shows it carrying blinds from Walthamstow depot outside Reading General Station.

No.175, another of Reading Corporation's six-wheelers, is seen at St. Mary Butts in the company of one of their Dennis Loline motor buses.

Older Reading four-wheeler No.138 is parked out of use outside their Mill Lane depot. It is one of twenty 59-seat BUT 9611Ts with Park Royal bodywork, new in 1949.

Six-wheeler No.170 is seen in Reading's Broad Street bound for Tilehurst. Most ironically, some twenty years after this picture was taken, ex-London Routemaster buses, many of which had replaced trolley-buses at home, were running on routes such as this in Reading.

No.186, one of Reading's 1961 Burlingham-bodied Sunbeams, is also seen bound for Tilehurst, crossing the River Kennett. This trolleybus is now preserved.

No.193, last of the same batch of twelve trolleybuses, heads out of the town on route 18. Fortunately, this trolleybus was also secured for preservation when the Reading system perished just thirteen months after this picture was taken.

Not far behind, No.174, one of the dozen Park Royal-bodied Sunbeam S7 six-wheelers, heads for Tilehurst on route 17. As mentioned earlier, this trolleybus survives in preservation today.

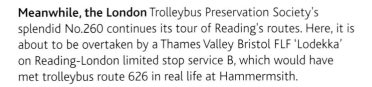

Meanwhile, the London Trolleybus Preservation Society's splendid No.260 continues its tour of Reading's routes. Here, it is about to be overtaken by a Thames Valley Bristol FLF 'Lodekka' on Reading-London limited stop service B, which would have met trolleybus route 626 in real life at Hammermsith.

Reading No.182, first of the batch of 1961 Burlingham-bodied Sunbeam F4As and also now preserved, heads for Tilehurst outside Reading Cemetery as one of the 1950 Park Royal-bodied S7s returns to the town centre. The complicated trolleybus overhead at this junction is of note.

Here is Reading's No.193 again, also passing Reading Cemetery, with preserved London Transport trolleybus No.260 following. It is bizarre to reflect that the London vehicle had already been in preservation for more than two years when this Reading trolleybus was built. It is also an ironic coincidence that Reading No.193 itself has survived in preservation!

At the same junction, preserved No.260's booms have to be manhandled onto the correct set of overhead to return towards London. Its blinds for route 660 are somewhat appropriate, as had there still been wiring for it to run beneath in London, it could have taken the wires for route 657 west of Hounslow, then continued via that route and then the 667 to Hammersmith. It had worked route 660 in real life to Hammersmith, of course.

One of the oldest surviving British trolleybuses is Hastings Tramways No.3, a Guy BTX with Dodson open-top, open-staircase 57-seat bodywork, new in April 1928. When Hastings' trolleybuses were abandoned following the system's takeover by Maidstone & District, it was equipped with a Commer engine to work seafront tours as a motor bus! This view sees it leaving the Brighton HCVC Rally on 5 May 1968.

At the same event, Brighton, Hove & District trolleybus No.6340, an AEC 661T with Weymann 54-seat bodywork, has returned home. It was new in September 1939, just in time for the outbreak of the Second World War, and remained in store for the duration, not entering service until hostilities had ceased. When this operator abandoned its trolleybuses in March 1959, it was initially preserved by the British Transport Commission and kept in the former London Transport bus garage at Clapham.

The ex-Huddersfield trolleybuses in use as public conveniences on Epsom Downs were still there on Derby Day 29/5/68 – this is the Gentlemens. Ironically, trolleybuses were still running in Huddersfield at this time, finally being abandoned in July 1968.

The only British trolleybus operator to make use of fairly new bodies on their trolleybuses after they were withdrawn was Doncaster Corporation. Their No.93 is a 1947 Leyland Titan PD2 originally carrying Leyland 56-seat bodywork, which has been refitted with a Roe 62-seat body built in 1958 to rebody one of a batch of utility Sunbeam W trolleybuses that had been acquired from Southend Corporation in 1954! It is seen in Doncaster's suburbs on 16 June 1968. Four of these Titans were so treated after Doncaster's trolleybus system was abandoned in December 1963.

Even more bizarre, the other five Roe bodies fitted to the ex-Southend trolleybuses were fitted to new Leyland Titan PD3 chassis for Doncaster Corporation! No.188, seen at their depot on the same day, is one of them. The thicker pillar between the nearside and offside forward windows gives the game away, having originally supported the trolleybuses' cabling. The cab area also looks rather clumsy where the originally full-fronted body had been cut away.

A visit to Bournemouth Corporation's Mallard Road depot on 14 July 1968 sees trolleybus No.272 still in service condition. It is a Sunbeam MF2B with Weymann 63-seat bodywork, and although only built in 1958, is one of the oldest examples still in service.

Of the same batch, No.263 is one of a group of these splendid, modern trolleybuses which have been dumped outside the depot for some two years.

Fellow 1958 Sunbeams Nos. 264, 258, 265 and 262 also make a sad sight dumped outside the depot. This view, when compared to the similar picture taken in January 1967, shows how they have now been cannibalised for spare parts, or maybe robbed by souvenir hunters.

Another visit to Bournemouth on 11 August 1968 finds 1959 Weymann-bodied Sunbeam MF2B No.278, first of the batch of ten delivered that year. It approaches The Square in the town centre. It overtakes the Corporation's 1960 Weymann-bodied Leyland Titan PD3/1 No.150.

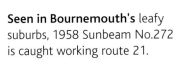

Seen in Bournemouth's leafy suburbs, 1958 Sunbeam No.272 is caught working route 21.

The penultimate trolleybus in Bournemouth's fleet, and thus also the penultimate one built for any British system, No.302, is also a Sunbeam MF2B but with Weymann 65-seat bodywork, delivered in October 1962. It is seen in Christchurch on route 20.

This is No.302 again, seen on the famous trolleybus turntable at Christchurch terminus. This was necessary, owing to the restricted street layout there precluding a turning circle or a loop around side streets, to enable trolleybuses to terminate and then return to the town centre.

Also in Christchurch, 1962 Sunbeam No.295 heads for the terminus. This final batch of British double-deck trolleybuses were also the only ones to carry reversed registrations.

All of Bournemouth's last trolleybus routes converged on The Square, where 1959 Sunbeam No.280 is seen arriving on route 21.

Also at The Square terminus, 1959 Sunbeam No.287 has arrived on route 23.

A last look at a trolleybus at Bournemouth's Mallard Road depot: 1959 Sunbeam No.285 clearly shows the open-platform rear entrance and front exit of these vehicles. As mentioned earlier, they could easily have been adapted for one-man operation, presumably with the rear entrance given doors and used as an exit. In the event, this trolleybus system was abandoned in April 1969.

A remarkable survivor still to be found in London on 31 August 1968 is all-Leyland class K2 trolleybus No.1201, rescued from George Cohen's Colindale scrapyard and used as a store shed at a garage just east of Shepherd's Bush Green – a short distance from where its fellows had run on route 657 from Isleworth depot on the final day more than six years before. This one, however, had last operated from Stamford Hill depot already, until withdrawal of trolleybuses there in July 1961.

Sadly, this is the last photograph I ever took of a trolleybus in service on Britain's streets. Caught from the front window of a Western Welsh bus en route from Barry to Cardiff on the evening of 22 September 1968, it is Cardiff Corporation No.280, one of thirteen BUT 9641T six-wheelers with East Lancs 72-seat bodywork built in 1955. They should have been good for several more years' service, but Cardiff's trolleybus system was abandoned in January 1970.

A remarkable sight at London's Brent Cross on 12 September 1971 is this very dilapidated trolleybus being towed southwards along the Hendon Way. It obviously has Weymann bodywork and has a faded blue and cream livery suggesting Bradford Corporation (whose system was still active at the time), but all signs of identity were removed. It is also not of the same batch of Weymann-bodied trolleybuses operated by Bradford and seen earlier in this book. I have never been able to establish its identity, or what happened to it. Can any readers help?

Although operation of trolleybuses in the United Kingdom ended in March 1972, several British trolleybuses would survive in continental Europe, for instance in Holland and Portugal. These, however, had been built for export, but in Spain, all but two of the 127 post-war Q1 class trolleybuses built for London Transport had been exported for further use. Most did indeed see service there, but by May 1976, when I travelled to Spain to photograph them, only two systems still had them in service. The largest was the important sea port of La Coruna where they ran on four different routes. This picture sees No.48 (ex-LT 1825) at the Los Castros terminus of route 2, which ran along the seafront to and from Puerta Real.

Also at Los Castros, Coruna No.36 (LT 1826) illustrates how these Q1s' bodies had been altered to offside (to British eyes!) loading, with a straight staircase being fitted on the nearside. Also clearly visible are the retrievers fitted to its booms.

This view of No.36 (1826) setting off from Los Castros for Puerta Real illustrates how on much of the Coruna system, trolleybus overhead was attached to roadside buildings rather than having its own dedicated traction standards. In Britain, such an arrangement would have involved complicated wayleave agreements!

As Coruna No.28 (1794) approaches Los Castros terminus, No.36 (1826) heads off in the distance towards the city centre. This view clearly shows how these Q1s also had a doored forward exit. Entry at the rear, which was also doored, was by a turnstile, similar to those on London's ill-fated MBS-type buses.

Also on route 2 bound for Los Castros, Coruna Tramways No.41 (1803) looks very smart having recently been repainted in their dark blue and cream livery, and as yet not defaced by advertisements. A close look at its front blind box reveals that the top aperture, where the route number had been shown in London, has been panelled over.

Another look at Coruna No.41 (1803), seen outside the city's main railway station, shows how these Q1s were also fitted with sturdy bumpers to protect them in the event of a collision. Also evident is a metal traction standard on the pavement behind the trolleybus.

In contrast, No.39 (1765) looks somewhat the worse for wear when seen near Coruna's harbour at the point where trolleybus routes 2, 3 and 12 intersected.

At route 2's Puerta Real terminus, trolleybus No.36 (1826) is seen arriving on the turning circle at the western end of Coruna's harbour. It makes an interesting contrast with the locally built single-deck bus on the left.

Also at the Puerta Real terminus, Coruna No.32 (1785) working route 2 has come to grief with a flat tyre, and has to be attended to by a fitter from the trolleybus depot, whose service van brings up the rear.

Coruna Tramways trolleybus route 3 also began at Puerta Real, paralleling route 2 half-way along the harbour front, and then turning inland to terminate at Ciudad Escolar. Working it here is No.46, which at first sight is hard to believe is a Q1 that has been cut down to become a single-decker! Although having the same entrance/exit arrangements as the double-deckers, it looks even odder owing to being repanelled to omit the cream band beneath its windows. Once LT No.1796, it passes Coruna's football stadium.

Double-deck trolleybuses also worked route 3, as seen by No.34 (1782) on its way to Ciudad Escolar. Of note here are the traction standards, and the modern housing in the background.

The same trolleybus is seen negotiating the turning circle at Ciudad Escolar terminus. The overhead wiring continuing beyond it is for access to the trolleybus depot, where all Coruna's Q1s were based.

Single-decker No.46 (1796) sets off from Puerta Real terminus for Ciudad Escolar as ugly tower blocks rise in the background.

Coruna route 10 was the third to terminate at Puerta Real. This ran inland to Los Mallos, on the way to which was a long, steep hill which was deemed too much for the double-deck Q1s to negotiate, hence a batch being cut down to single-deck. Perhaps a better solution might have been to fit the Q1s with run-back and coast brakes, as some of London's trolleybuses had for steep Highgate and Anerley Hills on routes 611 and 654 respectively? Here, No.40 (1815), another which has lost its below windows waistband, arrives at Puerta Real.

Another single-decker on route 10, seen at the Puerta Real terminus itself, No.43 (1777) retains the cream band beneath its windows, and contrasts with No.28 (1794) on route 2.

Similarly mutilated No.47 (1800) climbs the steep, cobbled hill that enforced single-deck operation to route 10's Los Mallos terminus.

At Los Mallos terminus itself, No.43 (1777) runs around the block to return to Puerta Real. A lasting memory I have of this place is that it absolutely stank of fish, presumably since La Coruna is a busy fishing port and the catches are processed here!

La Coruna's fourth route was the 12, running from Los Castros to Ciudad Escolar. This followed route 2 along as far as the seafront junction, from which it took up the route of the 3 to Ciudad Escolar. A smart No.30 (LT 1802) stands at Los Castros terminus.

Another look at No.30 (1802) heading from Ciduad Escolar towards Puerta Real in La Coruna's city centre.

Inside Coruna Tramways' Ciudad Escolar depot is No.27 (LT 1823) along with No.44 (1807), which has been cannibalised. Two other Q1s behind it have met a similar fate.

This view in Ciudad Escolar depot shows a group of Q1s that have been cut down to single-deck. No.45 is nearest the camera.

Inside the depot too, No.35 shows off its two sets of folding doors. Two cannibalised Q1s are just discernable behind it.

This view of a group of Q1s inside Ciudad Escolar depot shows how the rear ends of both double- and single-deck versions were altered for 'offside' loading.

Despite several of the Q1s looking very much the worse for wear, their depot was a modern and spacious building, with all the trolleybuses housed under cover as this picture shows. A modern single-deck motor bus is also just visible on the left.

Another operator which ran ex-London Transport Q1 trolleybuses into La Coruna was Coruna Carballo, which had run them on an inter-urban service between the two towns, involving fast running along country roads. Sadly, the system had closed in March 1971, but these two Q1s were still dumped at the Carballo depot.

OPPOSITE: A last look at the Coruna trolleybuses, where routes 2 and 10 part company near the harbour. Single-decker No.40 (LT1815) heads for Los Mallos, as a double-decker heads for Los Castros. La Coruna was to be the last Spanish town to operate ex-London trolleybuses, the last of which were finally withdrawn in January 1979. It is intriguing to speculate whether the Q1s would have lasted so long if they had been retained in London after all pre-war and wartime trolleybuses had been withdrawn. Maybe they could have done, bearing in mind that several of the earlier vehicles, notably the F1 class at Hanwell, lasted for as long as twenty-three years.

This Q1 at Carballo seems in slightly better shape, and illustrates how when they were in service, their blind boxes were completely panelled over. It is also noteworthy how warning lights were fitted on each side below the front upper-deck windows.

This rear view of another dumped Q1 shows how those with this operator, Trolebuses Coruna Carballona, to give it its full name, merely had a small rear-doored entrance on the offside.

The second Spanish operator still working ex-London Transport Q1 trolleybuses at this time was Pontevedra, who had just five of them. Here at their depot, their No.103 (LT No.1811) illustrates how their Q1s were rebuilt with offside platforms making a mirror image of how they looked in London. This one has seen better days, and they were withdrawn not long after these pictures were taken.

Similarly rebuilt No.102 (LT 1791) looks very careworn as it arrives at the terminus of route 2, the harbour town of Marin, close to the Portuguese border. Note how the original blind arrangement has been retained at the front.

The route between Pontevedra and Marin featured fast running alongside the spectacular scenery of the Ria Pontevedra Gorge, where No.101 (LT 1824) is seen here. Concrete traction standards and brackets support both sets of overhead on this stretch.

This view of No.101 (LT 1824), setting off from Marin for the fast run to Pontevedra, nicely shows the overhead and traction standards on this stretch of route.

Pontevedra trolleybus No.105 (LT1801) was rebuilt in a similar fashion to the Coruna Q1s, with an enclosed platform with folding doors as well as a front exit. It also appears to have had its staircase moved to a position behind the driver. This view on 3 June 1976 sees it arriving on the turning loop at Marin terminus.

Leaving the turning loop at the same point, No.101 (LT1824) heads back to Pontevedra. Its boom retrievers may be clearly seen in this picture, along with its conductor on the open platform.

No.105 (LT1801) approaches Pontevedra beside the gorge, and clearly shows the doored entrance and exit arrangement unique to this trolleybus in this fleet. The Galicia referred to in its rear advert refers to this part of Spain, not the Galicia in eastern Poland and the Ukraine which was notorious for the Tsarist pogroms of the late nineteenth and early twentieth centuries.

Closer to Pontevedra, No.101 (1824) still looks reasonably smart as it passes beneath an apparently disused railway line whose bridge is just high enough to allow double-deck trolleybuses to pass beneath it.

No.105 (LT1810) is about to pass beneath the same bridge on its way from Pontevedra to Marin. The small ex-RAC minivan just visible on the left belongs to a friend with whom I travelled to these operators in it.

This nearside (to British eyes) view of No.105 (1801) on the one-way loop in Marin shows how there are seats in the area where the platform and staircase had been on both decks, and that the staircase is in the front, behind the cab area on the nearside.

A general view of the small depot at Pontevedra, where there was covered accommodation for the double-deckers.

A last look at Q1s in Pontevedra, as No.105 (1801) arrives at the town centre trolleybus terminus. There were other trolleybus routes serving it, but they were foreign-built single-deckers.

A sad sight we encountered in Spain was a batch of nine Q1s, still in London Transport livery, which had been bought to replace trams in the town of Vigo. Never used in the event, they were boxed in to the town's former tram depot at Travesias by a new road development, as a result of which efforts to rescue and repatriate one failed. The one nearest the camera here still shows a Fulwell depot code!

This unfortunate Q1 had worked from the other depot to which they were delivered when new: Isleworth. As may be seen, over the fifteen years or so the trolleybuses had been here, they had been increasingly targeted by vandals.

A farewell shot of the eight complete Q1s, trapped inside the former Vigo tram depot at Travesias, where they were eventually broken up on site. Even those out of range from vandals throwing missiles from the roadside appear to have had their windows smashed!

OPPOSITE: Fortunately, a number of British trolleybuses have been preserved. One of the best known is London Transport C2 class No.260, which remarkably was rejected from LT's own museum collection, for which it had been saved in 1959, in favour of a later example in 1961! Thankfully, it was rescued from the scrapyard by the London Trolleybus Preservation Society's pioneer members Tony Belton and Fred Ivey. Here, in September 1978, it is somewhat ironically on show at the London Transport Museum when that entity had many of its exhibits housed at Syon Park. This immaculately restored trolleybus resides at the East Anglia Transport Museum, Carlton Colville, today.

Saddest of all was Q1 No.1787, which had been dropped on its back when unloaded at the docks in Spain, thereby crushing its rear end, staircase and platform. There was, however, one survivor from the Vigo trolleybuses – the tenth vehicle delivered there had been sold to Coruna Tramways to replace one of their fleet damaged in an accident. It had occupied the empty space between No.1787 and the other eight Q1s.

The pioneer London trolleybus, London United No.1 dating from 1931, was saved for posterity by London Transport after it had been replaced by new Q1 vehicles after the war. It was one of the permanent exhibits at Syon Park when seen here the same day, and survives in the LT Museum collection today. Its blind recalls when it made a farewell run on the last day of London's trolleybuses, ironically running from the depot at which it was new, Fulwell, in May 1962. For some reason, these early trolleybuses, whose design looked like a cross between a Feltham tram and contemporary LT and ST class motor buses of the day, were nicknamed 'Diddlers'.

Trolleybuses last ran in Islington in November 1961, and in this particular road in the borough, Goswell Road, in April 1959. However, the splendidly preserved London Transport C2 class trolleybus No.260 graced this thoroughfare on 8 July 1979, when it took part in a special cavalcade of London buses, past and present, which ran from London Wall to Hyde Park for a rally commemorating 150 years of London buses. It was, unfortunately but necessarily, on tow and here enters Goswell Road on the Islington, Angel, one-way system. This view shows the typical rear end design of London's trolleybuses, which was still clearly evident in the pictures earlier of the 'mirror image' converted Q1s in Pontevedra, Spain.

A commemorative event was held at Fulwell depot in May 1981 to mark the fiftieth anniversary of London's first trolley-buses. More's the pity they only lasted thirty-one years in London! One of London Transport's postwar Q1 class trolleybuses, No.1768 of the 1948 batch which replaced the 'Diddlers', was saved for the LT Museum and has returned to Fulwell for this event. As seen earlier, all but one of the other Q1s were exported to Spain.

Despite appearances suggesting the contrary earlier in this book, London trolleybus No.1201 survived its stint as a garage shed at Shepherd's Bush. Here, on 9 August 1981, it is seen at the East Anglia Transport Museum at Carlton Colville where it would eventually be restored to working order, as it is there today.

A number of non-London Trolleybuses have also been rescued by the London Trolleybus Preservation Society, and are housed and operated at Carlton Colville. On the same day as the previous picture, Ashton-Under-Lyne Corporation No.87, a BUT 9612T with Bond 60-seat bodywork new in 1956, accompanies Maidstone Corporation No.52, also a BUT but of the 9611T type with Weymann 56-seat bodywork. This had been new to the Brighton system in 1950 and acquired by Maidstone in 1959.

It is quite unusual to see trolleybuses at bus rallies, other than those held at either Carlton Colville or Sandtoft where working trolleybuses are kept. However, on 15 June 1986, splendid Bournemouth Corporation 1961 Weymann-bodied Sunbeam No.301, one of the very last double-deck trolleybuses built for use in Great Britain, is on display at a rally at Didcot.

On 6 July 1986, splendid London trolleybus No.260 gives rides at Carlton Colville and is already fifty years old. It never worked Bexleyheath route 696 in real life, however, always being based in North-West London!

For the fiftieth anniversary of the end of London's trolleybuses, a display of some of the survivors was staged at Fulwell depot. Here, Q1 No.1768 contrasts with 'Diddler' No.1 on 11 May 2012.

Also on display was London's official last working trolleybus, L3 class No.1521, now also in the care of the London Trolleybus Preservation Society and housed at Carlton Colville. When I photographed this vehicle at Fulwell on the last day, 8 May 1962, as seen earlier in this book, I had no idea that I would do so again fifty years later! I wonder how many of the other people in this photograph were at Fulwell on that sad day?

Part Three

A BRIEF LOOK AT TROLLEYBUS OPERATION IN THE UNITED KINGDOM

Bournemouth Corporation Weymann-bodied BUT 9641T trolleybus No.256, dating from 1950, heads a line up of its withdrawn fellows at their Mallard Road depot on 15 January 1967.

Although the British trolleybus is usually perceived to be an 'inter-war' phenomenon, when trolleybuses were a popular replacement for ageing tramway systems and were indeed in their heyday, trolleybuses had in fact been in use much earlier. As may be seen, some of the early systems were very short lived, yet ironically the city that had been the last to operate trolleybuses in this country, Bradford, was also the first where they operated, albeit on a joint service to Leeds which lasted only until 1928.

Below is a list of British trolleybus systems, in alphabetical order, showing their dates of introduction and withdrawal. Grateful thanks go to the British Trolleybus Society and the National Trolleybus Association for this information. The list is interspersed with a few photographs of trolleybuses working for some of the operators mentioned in their final years.

Aberdare: 15 January 1914 to 23 July 1925.
Ashton-Under-Lyne: 26 February 1935 to 31 December 1966.
Belfast: 28 March 1938 to 12 May 1968.
Birmingham: 27 November 1922 to 30 June 1951.

Bournemouth: 13 May 1933 to 20 April 1969.
Bradford: 20 June 1911 to 26 March 1972.
Brighton (Corporation): 1 May 1939 to 30 June 1961.
Brighton, Hove & District: 1 January 1945 to 24 March 1959.
Cardiff: 1 March 1942 to 11 January 1970.
Chesterfield: 25 May 1927 to 24 March 1938.
Cleethorpes: 18 July 1937 to 4 June 1960.
Darlington: 17 January 1926 to 31 July 1957.
Derby: 10 January 1932 to 9 September 1967.
Doncaster: 22 August 1928 to 14 December 1963.
Dundee: 3 September 1912 to 13 May 1914.
Glasgow: 3 April 1949 to 27 May 1967.
Grimsby: 3 October 1926 to 4 June 1960.
Halifax: 20 July 1921 to 24 October 1926.
Hartlepool: 28 July 1924 to 31 March 1953.
Hastings: 1 April 1928 to 31 May 1959.
Huddersfield: 4 December 1933 to 13 July 1968.
Ipswich: 2 September 1923 to 23 August 1963.
Keighley (Cedes Stoll): 3 May 1913 to 3 May 1926.
Keighley (Standard): 20 August 1924 to 31 August 1932.
Kingston-Upon-Hull: 25 July 1937 to 31 October 1964.
Leeds: 20 June 1911 to 26 July 1928.

Bournemouth was the last British operator to have new trolleybuses delivered, as late as 1962. Typical of these was No.282, a Sunbeam MF2B with Weymann dual-entrance bodywork new in 1959. It is seen in Christchurch on 11 August 1968, eleven months before the system was abandoned.

Seen on 7 October 1967 amid redevelopment in the city centre, Bradford 778 is typical of many trolleybuses the Corporation acquired from other operators. It is a Karrier W new to Llanelli Corporation in 1945, and acquired by Bradford in 1958 and given a new East Lancs body.

By pure chance, I was able to photograph the very last trolleybus to run home to a North London depot on its final day in service, 2 January 1962. This was MCCW-bodied AEC chassissless L3 class No.1468 seen at Craven Park heading homewards around lunchtime that day on route 660. It would bring to an end trolleybus operation in my part of London in the early hours of Wednesday, 3 January when it ran in from this route to Finchley depot.

Trolleybuses usually lasted longer than motor buses, but here on 3 October 1965, Nottingham Corporation 1950 Brush-bodied BUT 9641T No.526 is one of several dating only from the early 1950s that await disposal in the yard of one of their depots. The system closed at the end of June 1966 – ironically trams and not trolleybuses have returned to the city since!

Llanelli: 26 December 1932 to 8 November 1952
London: 16 May 1931 to 8 May 1962.
Maidstone: 1 May 1928 to 15 April 1967.
Manchester: 1 March 1938 to 31 December 1966.
Mexborough & Swinton: 31 August 1915 to 26 March 1961.
Newcastle-Upon-Tyne: 2 October 1935 to 2 October 1966.
Nottingham: 10 April 1927 to 30 June 1966.
Notts & Derby: 7 January 1932 to 25 April 1953.
Oldham: 26 August 1925 to 3 September 1926.
Pontypridd: 18 September 1930 to 31 January 1957.
Portsmouth: 4 August 1934 to 27 July 1963.
Ramsbottom: 14 August 1913 to 31 March 1931.
Reading: 18 July 1936 to 3 November 1968.
Rhondda: 22 December 1914 to 10 March 1915.
Rotherham: 3 October 1912 to 2 October 1965.
St. Helens: 11 July 1927 to 30 June 1958.
Southend-On-Sea: 16 October 1925 to 28 October 1954.

South Lancashire: 3 August 1930 to 31 October 1958.
South Shields: 12 October 1936 to 29 April 1964.
Stockport: 10 March 1913 to 11 September 1920.
Teesside: 8 November 1919 to 18 April 1971.
Walsall: 22 July 1931 to 3 October 1970.
Wigan: 7 May 1925 to 30 September 1931.
Wolverhampton: 29 October 1923 to 5 March 1967.
York (First operation): 22 December 1920 to 31 December 1929.
York (Second operation): 6 October 1931 to 5 January 1935.

A study of the dates of operation does bear out that the heyday of the trolleybus was in the inter-war years, especially the 1930s, which is quite natural considering that in this period, early electric tramway systems were becoming due for updating, and the trolleybus was seen as the way ahead.

Although some systems, notably Bournemouth and Reading, bought new trolleybuses and also

L3 class trolleybuses also comprised the whole of Fulwell depot's allocation at the very end of trolleybus operation in London. This one, awaiting departure for the evening rush hour on the last day, 8 May 1962, appears to carry blinds not only for Fulwell's own routes (601, 602, 603, 604, 605 and 667) but also route 657, usually Isleworth's service. Have the other young lads in the picture 'bunked' school as I had?

Reading Corporation Park Royal-bodied BUT 9611T four-wheeler No.138, the first of twenty delivered in 1949, stands outside their Mill Lane depot on 8 October 1967, just over a year before the abandonment of this system.

extended their systems into the early 1960s, it is again apparent that the 'writing was on the wall' for the British trolleybus after the Second World War ended, when, perhaps following London Transport's lead, surviving tram systems were usually replaced by motor buses, as increasingly also were the trolleybuses themselves in the 1950s and 1960s. Indeed, the only operator to introduce an entirely new trolleybus system after the war was Glasgow City Transport, and even this did not fully replace their trams, which survived until 1962.

Also noteworthy is the fact that most operators were municipal systems; that is those owned and operated by the relevant town or city councils. However, the biggest of all was London Transport, a publicly owned body which had taken over both company and municipal tramway systems in and around the metropolis in 1933. It followed on from the initiative of London United Tramways by setting out to replace all of its trams by trolleybuses, including the huge system inherited from the London County Council. More's the pity that the Second World War stopped this plan from being completed!

It is fortunate that many operators, London Transport included, saw fit to preserve some of their trolleybuses for posterity. My two little daughters, Felicity (left) and Margaret (right), stand in front of LT's No.1253 in the London Transport Museum in August 1987. This was one of more than three hundred all-Leyland K-types in their fleet, typical of the London Transport trolleybuses delivered in 1938/39 as the storm clouds of war gathered over Europe. The LT trolleybus emblem on its cab, which all of their fleet carried front and rear, is particularly striking. Most EXV-registered trolleybuses, 379 in all, ran in my local North London area.